P9-EMP-964

DISCARD

Rocks and Minerals

Kathleen Weidner Zoehfeld

NATIONAL
GEOGRAPHIC

Washington, D.C.

For my Grandad, who loved the rocks of the Catskills
—K. W. Z.

A special thanks to Steve Tomecek, a.k.a. "The Dirtmeister,"
for lending us his expertise in the creation of this book

Design by YAY! Design

Paperback ISBN: 978-1-4263-1038-6
Library edition ISBN: 978-1-4263-1039-3

Photo Credits

Cover, Dorling Kindersley/Getty Images; 1, Walter Geiersperger/Corbis; 2, Pablo Romero/Shutterstock; 4-5, Michael DeYoung/ Corbis; 6-7, Allen Donilkowski/Flickr RF/Getty Images; 8, Suzi Nelson/Shutterstock; 9 (top left), Martin Novak/Shutterstock; 9 (top right), Manamana/Shutterstock; 9 (left center), Tyler Boyes/Shutterstock; 9 (right center), Biophoto Associates/Photo Researchers, Inc.; 9 (bottom left), Charles D. Winters/Photo Researchers RM/Getty Images; 9 (bottom right), Steffen Foerster Photography/Shutterstock; 10, Dorling Kindersley/Getty Images; 11 (top), Charles D. Winters/Photo Researchers RM/Getty Images; 11 (bottom), Biophoto Associates/Photo Researchers, Inc.; 12, Suzi Nelson/Shutterstock; 12-13, Tim Robinson; 14 (top), Bragin Alexey/Shutterstock; 14 (center), Visuals Unlimited/Getty Images; 14 (bottom), Glen Allison/Photodisc/Getty Images; 15, beboy/ Shutterstock; 16, Jim Lopes/Shutterstock; 16 (inset), Suzi Nelson/Shutterstock; 17 (bottom), Visuals Unlimited/Getty Images; 17 (top), Gary Ombler/Dorling Kindersley/Getty Images; 18 (bottom right), Doug Martin/Photo Researchers/Getty Images; 18, Suzi Nelson/Shutterstock; 19 (top left), Michal Baranski/Shutterstock; 19 (top right), Tyler Boyes/Shutterstock; 19 (bottom left), Charles D. Winters/Photo Researchers RM/Getty Images; bottom right: 19 (bottom right), Doug Martin/Photo Researchers RM/Getty Images; 19 (bottom), A. Louis Goldman/Photo Researchers, Inc.; 20 (top left), sculpies/Shutterstock; 20 (top right), David W. Hughes/Shutterstock; 20 (bottom), Philippe Psaila/Photo Researchers, Inc.; 21 (top left), S.J. Krasemann/Peter Arnold/Getty Images; 21 (top right), Myotis/Shutterstock; 21 (bottom left), Mark A Schneider/Photo Researchers/Getty Images; 21 (bottom right), Jim Parkin/Shutterstock; 22-23, Tim Robinson; 24, Dorling Kindersley/Getty Images; 25, James L. Amos/Photo Researchers RM/ Getty Images; 26 (bottom left), Mr. Lightman/Shutterstock; 27 (top left),Breck P. Kent/Animals Animals; 27 (top right), Burazin/ Getty Images; 27 (bottom left), Biophoto Associates/Photo Researchers RM/Getty Images; 27 (bottom right), Don Farrall/Getty Images/SuperStock; 28, SuperStock; 29, Gary Blakeley/Shutterstock; 30 (top), beboy/Shutterstock; 30 (center), Dr. Marli Miller/ Visuals Unlimited, Inc./Getty Images; 30 (bottom), Dan Shugar/Aurora Photos; 31 (top left), Cbonjasuwan/Shutterstock; 31 (top right), Bakalucha/Shutterstock; 31 (bottom left), Leene/Shutterstock; 31 (bottom right), Buquet Christophe/Shutterstock; 32 (top right), Dan Shugar/Aurora Photos; 32 (top left), Martin Novak/Shutterstock; 32 (center right), beboy/Shutterstock; 32 (center left), Bragin Alexey/Shutterstock; 32 (bottom right), Jim Lopes/Shutterstock; 32 (bottom left), LesPalenik/Shutterstock; header, HamsterMan/Shutterstock; background, sommthink/Shutterstock

Printed in the United States of America
12/WOR/1

Table of Contents

Rocks Are Everywhere

Walk outside and look around. You may see rocks right under your feet. Are they gray or black, tan or brown? They might be green, blue, white, pink, or even red.

Or maybe they sparkle with lots of different colors!

Pick up the rocks. Do they feel
smooth or rough? Are they heavy
to hold? Or do they feel light

in your hands? Rocks
look and feel the way they do
because of the minerals in them.

Amazing Minerals

All rocks are made up of minerals. Each mineral has its own special shape, called a crystal (KRIS-tal).

Geologists (jee-OL-uh-jists) have found many minerals on Earth. Some minerals are easy to find. Others are hard to find.

Words Rock

CRYSTAL: The shape a mineral takes in a rock when the rock forms

GEOLOGIST: A scientist who studies rocks

Easy to Find

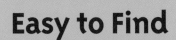

quartz

mica

feldspar

Hard to Find

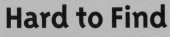

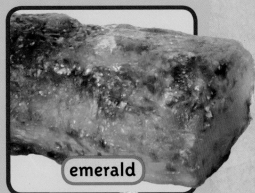
emerald

sapphire

gold

Mineral Mash-Up

Some rocks are made of just one mineral. But most rocks are made of two or more.

The mineral gold is often mixed with quartz.

Limestone is made of one mineral.

Pegmatite (PEG-muh-tite) is made of many minerals.

Rock Groups

Rocks can form in three different ways. So geologists put rocks in three groups:

1. **Igneous** (IG-nee-us)

2. **Sedimentary** (SED-uh-MEN-ter-ee)

3. **Metamorphic** (met-uh-MOR-fik)

Words Rock

IGNEOUS ROCKS: Rocks that are formed by the cooling of super hot rocks

MAGMA: Hot, melted rock that forms inside the Earth and comes out as lava

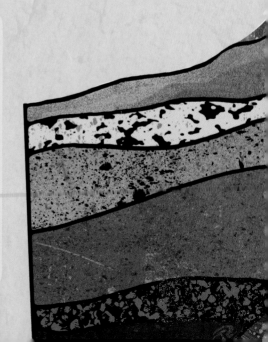

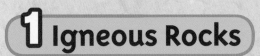

1 Igneous Rocks

Most of the rocks on our planet are igneous rocks. Igneous rocks begin to form deep inside the Earth. Here the rock is very hot. It is called magma (MAG-muh).

lava

volcano

magma

Granite (GRAN-it) forms when magma cools slowly underground.

Obsidian (ob-SID-ee-an) forms when lava cools quickly above ground.

Magma turns into igneous rock when it cools. Sometimes magma cools slowly underground.

When volcanoes erupt, magma pushes up from underground. Above ground, it cools quickly.

These basalt rocks in Ireland were formed millions of years ago by lava from a volcano.

Magma that flows from a volcano is called lava.

Sandstone is made up of grains of sand.

Words Rock

SEDIMENTARY ROCKS: Rocks that are formed when many small pieces of rock are glued together

2 Sedimentary Rocks

Rocks are broken into small pieces by wind, rain, and ice. These pieces are called sediment.

Shale is made of layers of mud pressed together.

Sediment is washed or blown into lakes and oceans. The sediment sinks. It builds up in layers on the bottom.

Conglomerate (con-GLOM-ur-it) is made of many things, including sand and pebbles.

Minerals mixed in the water glue the rock together. This is one way sedimentary rock is formed.

③ Metamorphic Rocks

On Earth we stand on huge slabs of rock called tectonic (tek–TON–ik) plates. These plates are always moving, but most of the time we can't feel them move.

When plates move past each other or crash into each other, the rocks are heated up and squeezed. This changes the rocks. They become metamorphic rocks.

Words Rock

METAMORPHIC ROCKS: Rocks that have been changed through heating and squeezing

Sandstone (sedimentary) becomes quartzite (metamorphic).

Limestone (sedimentary) becomes marble (metamorphic).

Folded metamorphic rock layers in Italy

7 Cool Rock Facts

2 Diamonds are the hardest minerals on Earth. They can even cut steel.

1 The ancient Egyptians built the pyramids with limestone thousands of years ago. They still stand today.

3 The softest mineral in the world is talc. You can crumble it with your fingers.

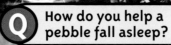

4

Some pumice rocks are so light they float on water.

5

The moon is made mostly of igneous rock.

6

A geode looks like a plain dull rock on the outside. Crack it open and there might be beautiful crystals hidden inside.

7

Obsidian feels as smooth as glass.

21

The Rock Cycle

Our Earth is like one giant rock factory. Old rocks are breaking into smaller and smaller pieces. New rocks are forming all the time.

On Earth, some things happen over and over again in the same order. This is called a cycle.

igneous rocks

igneous rocks

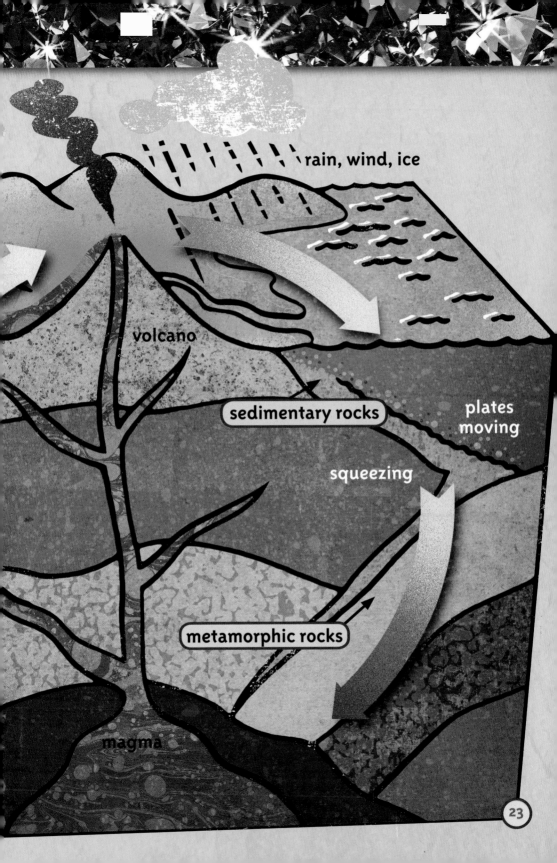

rain, wind, ice

volcano

sedimentary rocks

plates moving

squeezing

metamorphic rocks

magma

Fossils

Sometimes shells, bones, or other parts of living things get covered in sediment. Water seeps into tiny spaces in the bones or shells.

Minerals in the water are left behind. The bones or shells turn into fossils (FOS–uls). Fossils can be found in some sedimentary rocks.

A shell fossil

A scientist at work taking dinosaur bones out of rock

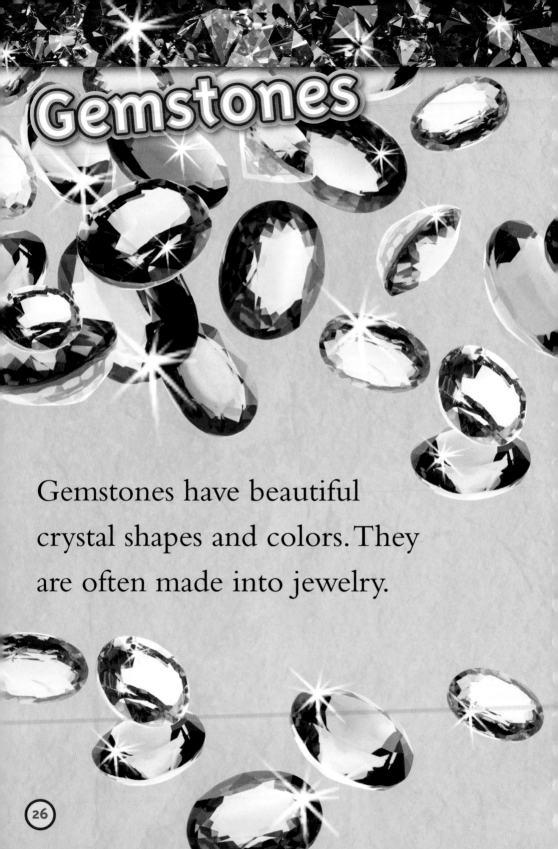

Gemstones

Gemstones have beautiful crystal shapes and colors. They are often made into jewelry.

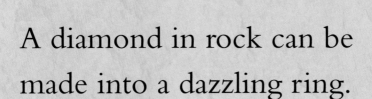

A diamond in rock can be made into a dazzling ring.

diamond

A ruby in rock is cleaned and cut. Then it is a gem!

ruby

Here to Stay

Look around you at the buildings and roads. Do you see rocks? They are everywhere!

Bricks are made of clay minerals.

Steps can be made of sandstone.

Limestone can be used to make concrete for sidewalks.

The walls of the Washington Monument are made mostly of white marble. The monument is the tallest stonework structure in the world.

Many things we build with rocks will still be standing years and years from now.

Stump Your Parents

Can your parents answer these questions about rocks? You might know more than they do!

Answers are at the bottom of page 31.

What comes out of a volcano?

A. pebbles
B. lava
C. sediment
D. water

The cycle of old rocks turning into new rocks is called _____.

A. the mineral cycle
B. the sedimentary cycle
C. the fossil cycle
D. the rock cycle

What do you call a scientist who studies rocks?

A. an astronomer
B. a biologist
C. a rock star
D. a geologist

4

In what type of rock can you sometimes find fossils?

A. igneous
B. sedimentary
C. metamorphic
D. lava

5

Beautiful rock crystals can be made into ____.

A. glitter
B. rock candy
C. gems
D. toys

6

What are rocks made of?

A. minerals
B. seeds
C. living things
D. wood

7

What gives a rock, like this piece of malachite, its color?

A. minerals
B. paint
C. seaweed
D. crayons

CRYSTAL: The shape a mineral takes in a rock when the rock forms

GEOLOGIST: A scientist who studies rocks

IGNEOUS ROCKS: Rocks that are formed by the cooling of super hot rocks

MAGMA: Hot, melted rock that forms inside the Earth and comes out as lava

METAMORPHIC ROCKS: Rocks that have been changed through heating and squeezing

SEDIMENTARY ROCKS: Rocks that are formed when many small pieces of rock are glued together